A New True Book

HEREDITY

By Dennis Fradin

Consultant: Steve S. Sommer, M.D., Ph.D.
Department of Biochemistry
and Molecular Biology
Mayo Clinic

CHILDRENS PRESS®
CHICAGO

This young girl inherited her red hair and freckles from her mother.

For Dear Aunt Carolyn Abrahams

Library of Congress Cataloging-in-Publication Data

Fradin, Dennis B.
  Heredity.

  (A New true book)
  Includes index.
  Summary: Presents basic information on heredity, discussing such topics as chromosomes, genes, and multiple births.
  1. Genetics—Juvenile literature. 2. Heredity—Juvenile literature. [1. Genetics. 2. Heredity] I. Title.
QH437.5.F73 1987   575.1   87-831
ISBN 0-516-01233-9

Childrens Press, Chicago
Copyright ©1987 by Regensteiner Publishing Enterprises, Inc.
All rights reserved. Published simultaneously in Canada.
Printed in the United States of America.
1 2 3 4 5 6 7 8 9 10 R 96 95 94 93 92 91 90 89 88 87

PHOTO CREDITS

© Cameramann International, Ltd.—9 (right), 12 (left), 14, 23 (left), 30 (right), 31 (left), 37 (left)

© Camerique/H. Armstrong Robert—9 (left), 41 (right)

Marilyn Gartman Agency:
© Lee Balterman—45 (bottom)
© Spencer Grant—4 (top left)
© Michael Phillip Manheim—37 (right)
© Frank Siteman—8 (left)

Courtesy Genex Corporation—25 (left), 68 (2 photos)

© Jerry Hennen—39 (right)

Historical Pictures Service, Chicago—15 (2 photos), 16 (left)

© Bob Skelly/Image Finders—19 (left)

Journalism Services:
© Paul E. Burd—28
© John Patsch—38
SIU—19 (right), 20, 33 (2 photos), 43

Nawrocki Stock Photo:
© Robert Amft—44 (top)
© Larry Brooks—23 (right)
© Jerry Howard—39 (left)
© Ken Sexton—4 (top right)
© Les Van—10 (right)
© Jim Whitmer—12 (middle)
© Will Fields—34 (right)

Photri—Cover, 8 (right), 17 (left), 30 (left)
© A. Novak—4 (bottom)
© L. Howe—7

© H. Armstrong Roberts—34 (left)

R.L. Brinster & R.E. Hammer, School of Veterinary Medicine, University of Pennsylvania—27

Tom Stack & Associates:
© Alan D. Briere—11
© Brian Parker—10 (left)
© Tom Stack—2

© Lynn Stone—12 (right), 31 (right)

Tom Dunnington—16, 29

Cover: Identical twins

TABLE OF CONTENTS

What Is Heredity?...5

Cats Have Kittens, Dogs Have Puppies...7

Each Individual Is Unique...12

The Heredity Seekers...15

It's in the Genes!...18

What Are Genes Made Of?...24

How Do Genes Work?...26

Half from Mom, Half from Dad...30

Multiple Births...36

Genetic Diseases...40

Words You Should Know...46

Index...48

Children inherit the color of their eyes and hair from their parents.

WHAT IS HEREDITY?

Heredity is the passing of traits from parents to their young. The traits are passed on to the offspring when the parents reproduce. Your eye color is a trait that is due to your heredity. Your hair color and looks were also passed to you by your parents.

All living things obey the laws of heredity. That is because each animal and plant was produced by an earlier generation. Even tiny bacteria, which reproduce by splitting in half, pass their traits on to the new bacteria.

Heredity works in two ways. It makes each living thing resemble others of its kind in many ways. It also helps make each living thing one of a kind.

CATS HAVE KITTENS, DOGS HAVE PUPPIES

Thanks to heredity, all living things resemble others of their kind in some ways. To begin with, each living thing gives birth to its own kind. Cats have kittens, dogs have

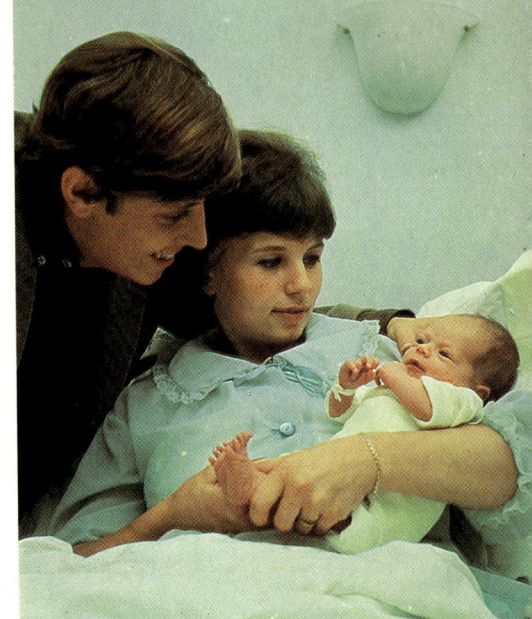

Each living thing gives birth to its own kind.

puppies, people have baby humans, and oak trees have little oaks. No mouse has given birth to a whale, and no human will ever give birth to an oak tree!

Plants and animals also look like others of their kind. Nearly all people are born with one head, two

Parents pass on traits, such as skin color and shape of the eye or eyelids, to their children.

arms, and two legs. On the other hand, most species (types) of starfish have five arms. Living things share a basic size with their own kind, too. Compared to people, all mice are small and all elephants are large.

Starfish growing three new arms (left) and sunflowers (right)

Each kind of living creature also has special traits. Starfish can grow new arms when their old ones are cut off. Sunflowers can turn so that they face the sun all day. Many species of birds have the instinct to fly hundreds of miles to the same spot each winter.

Canada geese migrate every year.

Finally, although plants cannot think, each type of animal has a basic mental ability. Some people are "smarter" than others, but all people are smarter than goldfish. All dogs have better brains than worms have. If you don't believe it, try teaching a worm to roll over!

EACH INDIVIDUAL IS UNIQUE

How interesting would life be if all people were exactly alike? Fortunately, heredity also helps make

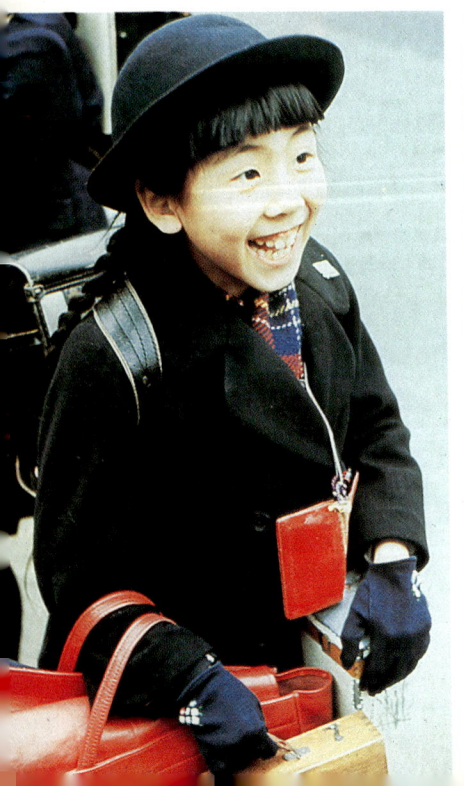
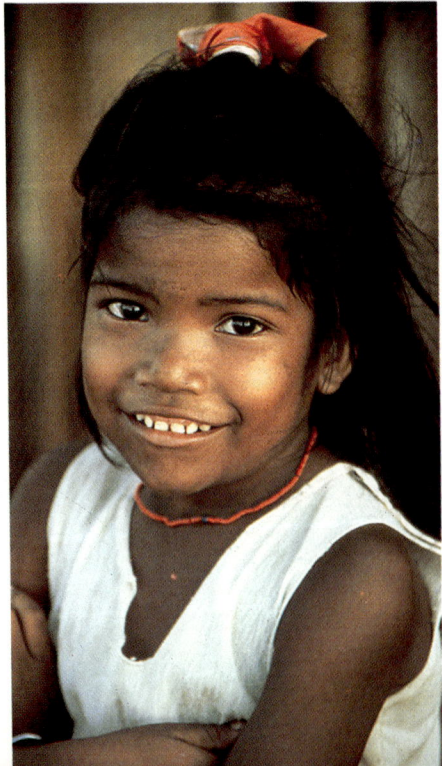
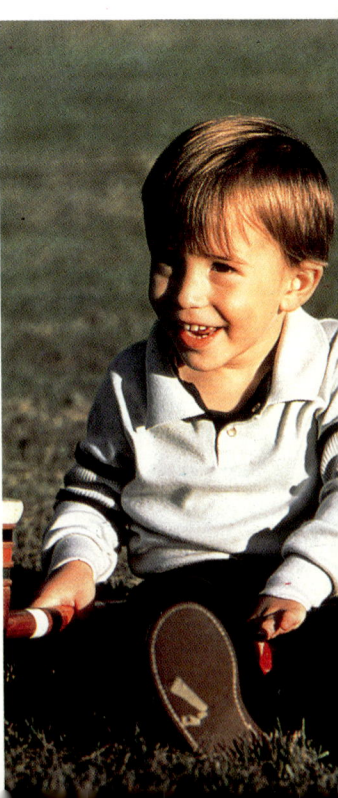

each member of a species unique.

Unless you have an identical twin, no one else looks exactly like you. And even identical twins vary in personality. Each plant and animal is also unique. Most dog and cat owners could pick their pets out of all the other dogs and cats on Earth. Each tree, earthworm, and butterfly also has special qualities.

Another factor besides heredity helps make each

These brothers may look alike, but their heredity and environment have made them different.

living thing unique. This is environment—a living thing's surroundings. For example, your heredity is one reason why you differ from your brother or sister. Your environment has also helped make you one of a kind. You have had different teachers, friends, and experiences than your sister or brother has had.

THE HEREDITY SEEKERS

For most of history, people did not know what governed heredity. Many thought that something in the blood determined it. Only in the past 150 years have scientists helped solve the mystery.

Matthais Schleiden (1804-1881)

During the 1830s the German scientists Matthias Schleiden and Theodor Schwann showed that plants and animals are made of tiny units called cells. An Austrian monk, Gregor

Theodor Schwann (1810-1882)

Gregor Johann Mendel (1822-1844)

MENDEL'S PEA PLANT EXPERIMENTS

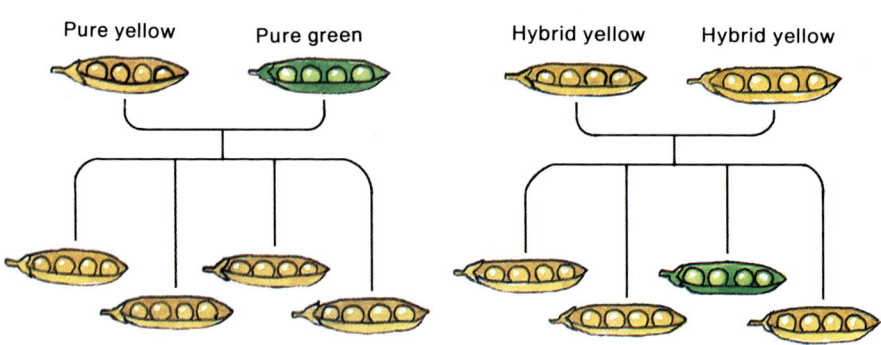

Mendel learned that the yellow seed color was the dominant trait in this experiment that mated a pure yellow seed with a pure green seed. The offspring plants were yellow hybrids. They had traits of the green plant in them.

Mendel discovered that the yellow hybrid seeds produced one green plant to three yellow plants. This was an important step in understanding how traits get passed from one generation to the next.

Johann Mendel, learned many rules of heredity by experimenting with pea plants during the mid-1800s. Then, in the late 1800s and early 1900s powerful microscopes helped scientists learn

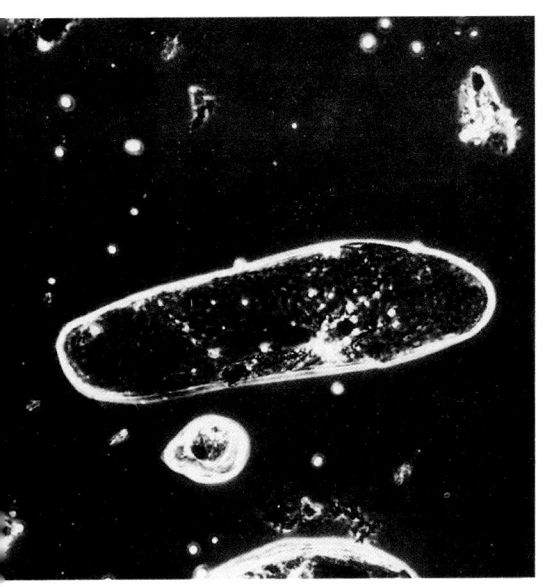 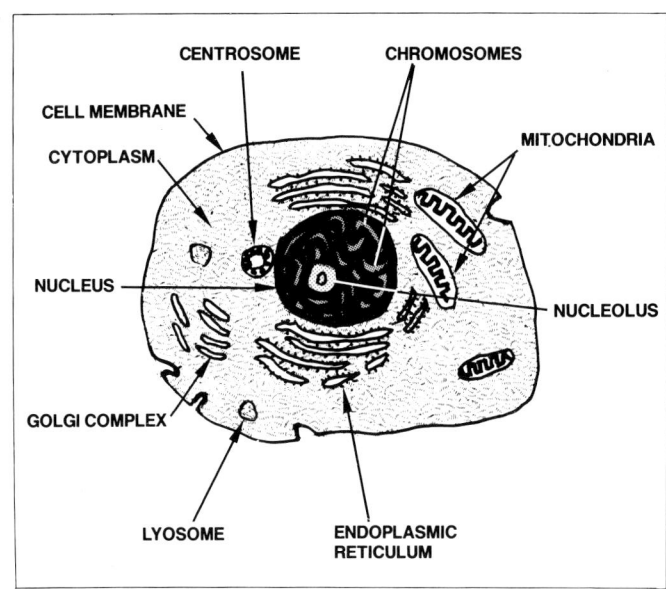

Photograph of slipper-shaped single cell (left) shows the nucleus in lower right center. The drawing (right) shows the parts of a cell. The nucleus, or center, is where DNA is stored.

what it is within cells that determines heredity.

Inside each cell are tiny structures called chromosomes. Each chromosome has numerous units called genes on it. The genes determine heredity.

IT'S IN THE GENES!

All living things are made of cells. Most cells are so small that they can only be seen through a microscope. A bacterium is made of just one cell. Higher life forms have many cells. Your body has about 100 trillion (100,000,000,000,000) cells.

Cells of various kinds of plants and animals look much alike. Your cells are

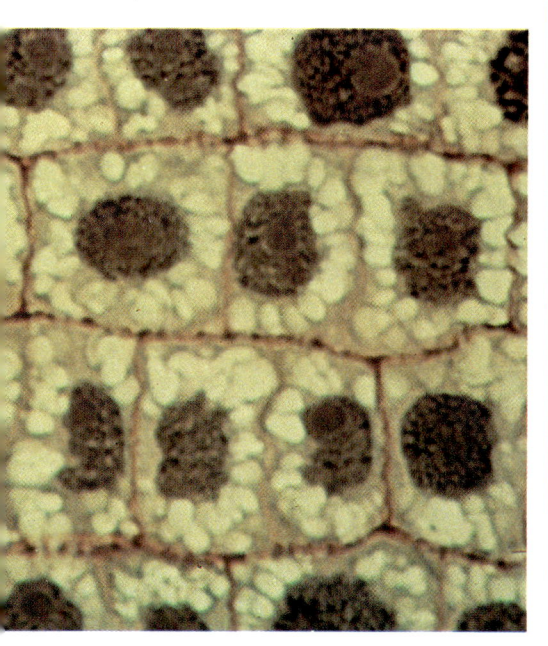
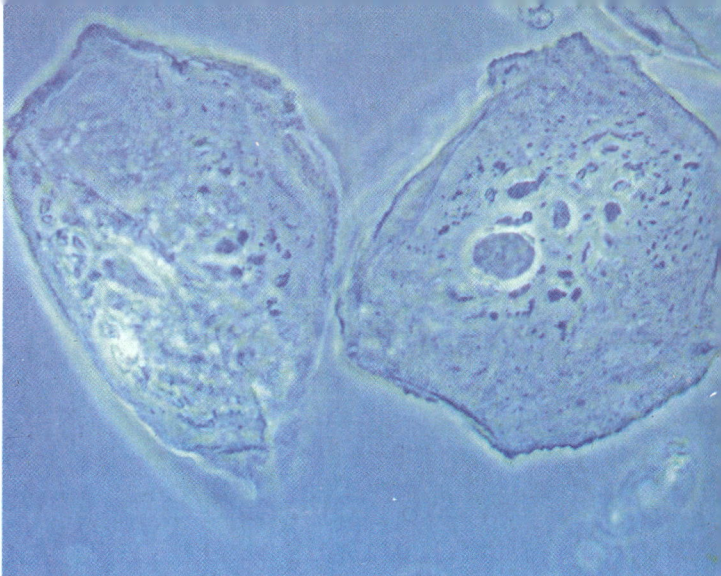

Square plant cells (left) with central nucleus. Human cheek cells (above) not very different from those of a cat or tree. But cells contain material that makes one organism a cat, another a tree, and a third a person. This material is in the nucleus, a control center inside of each cell.

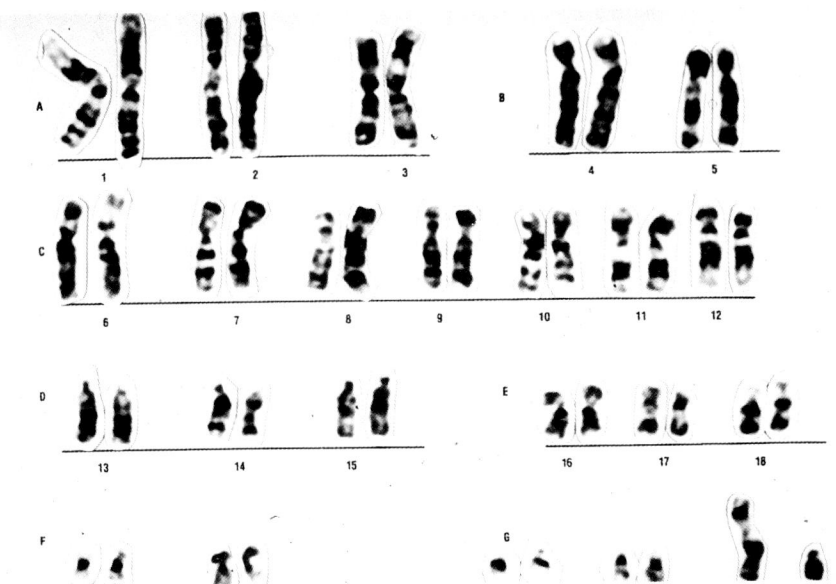

This magnified picture shows human chromosomes. The chromosomes, in the nucleus of the cell, contain all the genetic information of the cell.

Within the nucleus are chromosomes. These chromosomes are so small that thousands of human ones laid end to end would only be an inch long. Each species has a certain number of chromosomes in each body cell. A human being has 46, a tomato has 24, a pea plant has 14, and a gorilla has 48 chromosomes in each body cell.

The chromosome number is always even because chromosomes occur in pairs in body cells. Human beings have two sets of 23 chromosomes in each cell, making the total 46. A pea plant has two sets of seven, making the total 14.

Chromosomes can have thousands of genes. If you think of a chromosome as a bead bracelet, a gene is somewhat like a single bead. Genes determine heredity. You have one brain and two arms because genes told your body to develop that way.

Your nose is two inches instead of two feet long because genes told it when to stop growing. Special genes helped you develop your own unique personality.

All humans have 46 chromosomes in each body cell. Most human chromosomes have more than a thousand genes on them.

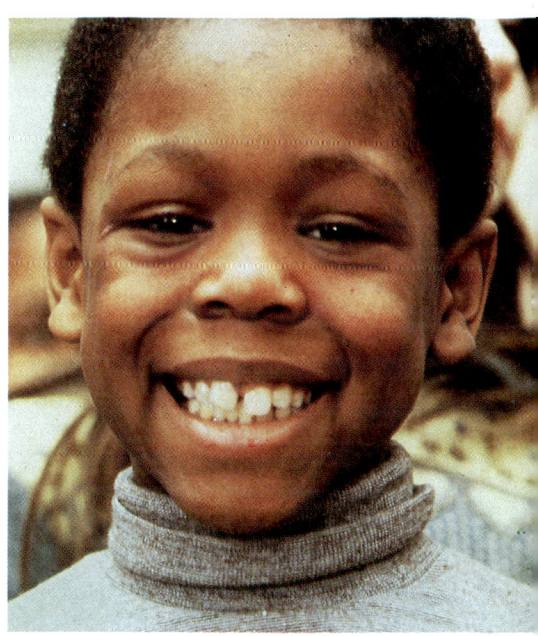

WHAT ARE GENES MADE OF?

Although tiny, genes are quite complex. They are made mainly of deoxyribonucleic acid. Geneticists (scientists who study heredity) call this vital substance DNA for short. DNA is called "the code of life" because it is the main gene material.

All DNA is not alike. There are chemical differences in DNA structure from gene to

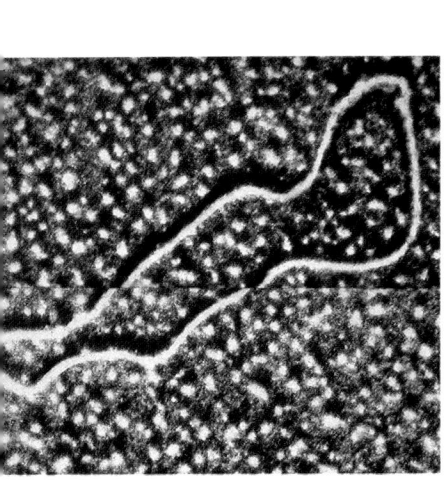 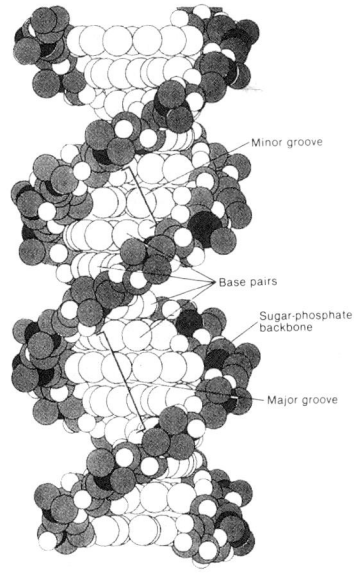 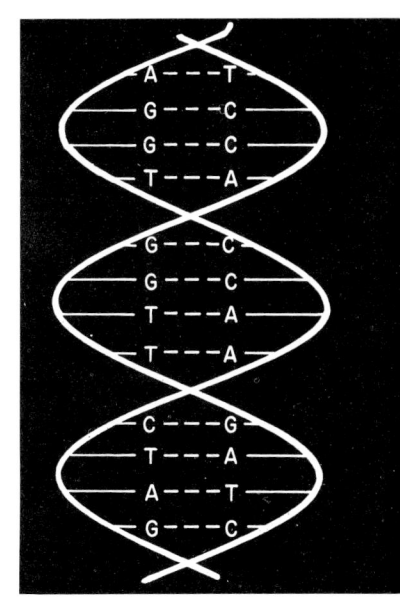

DNA (left) has been photographed through a microscope. Scientists have built models of DNA to show its parts. The model at right shows how the compounds that are the basic structural units of DNA are arranged. The As in one chain are always linked to the Ts in the other. The Gs in one to the Cs in the other.

gene. This is why genes vary. Each person has about 50,000 genes. Chemical differences cause some genes to control eye color, others to control height, and still others to control intelligence.

HOW DO GENES WORK?

At the start of life, genes told your body to grow one head, two eyes, and one mouth. They also tell the body what substances to make throughout life. Genes do all this by directing cells to produce special substances called proteins. Each gene contains the blueprint for producing its own special protein. In turn, each protein directs a certain bodily activity.

Each of your body cells contains all of your 50,000 genes. This means that the genes that told your brain to develop are also located on your nose cells. Toe-growing genes are

The supermouse at right is so big because it was given the human growth-hormone gene.

also found in your stomach cells. Why, then, didn't you grow brains on your nose or toes in your stomach?

The answer is that genes can be switched on and off. While the brain is growing, the brain-growing

genes are switched on in the head but are off elsewhere. Geneticists do not know exactly how this switching system works. But we should be grateful for it. Would you want to have an eye growing in your navel, or a tooth on your hand?

HALF FROM MOM, HALF FROM DAD

You are somewhat like your father and somewhat like your mother. That is because one cell from your mother joined with one cell from your father to make you. In other

words, part of your heredity came from your mother and part came from your father. It works this way with many animals and plants.

The special cells that made you are called sex cells. The sex cell from the father is called a sperm. The one from the mother is called an egg.

A person's sex cells differ from all of his or her other cells. Each body cell has 46 chromosomes—two sets of 23. An egg cell has just one set of 23 chromosomes. A sperm also has just 23 chromosomes.

When sperm and egg unite, the 23 chromosomes from the sperm join with the 23 in the egg. The fertilized egg (which will grow into a person) then

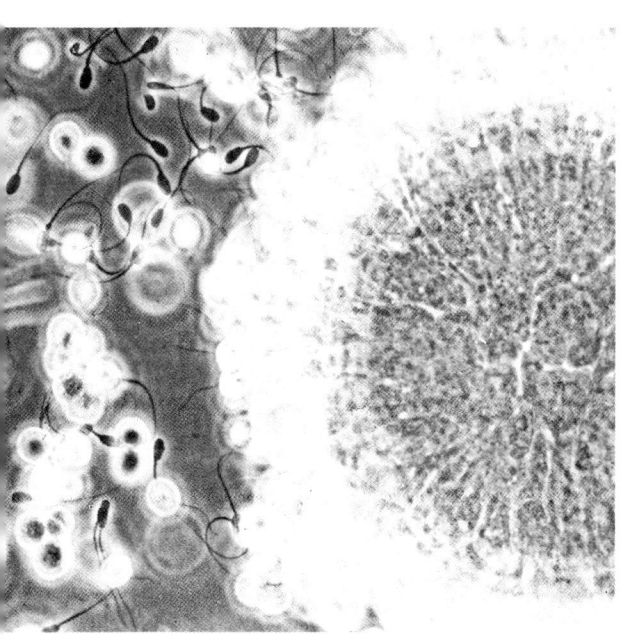
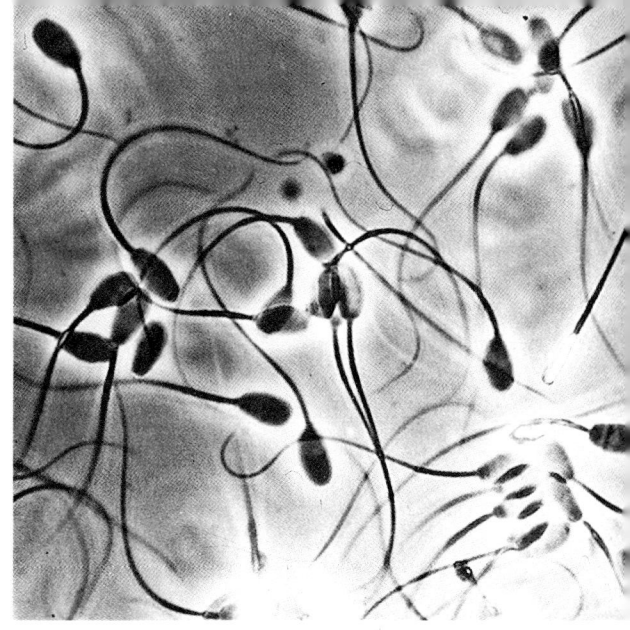

Egg with sperm (left) and sperm (above)

has 46 chromosomes. Half are from the father, and half are from the mother. The genes on those chromosomes determine the new person's traits.

Genes work in pairs. However, in many cases both members of the pair

Eye color (left) and the ability to roll one's tongue (right) are caused by genes.

are not equal. Say that a child gets a gene for brown eyes from one parent, and a gene for blue eyes from the other parent. The child will have brown eyes. The reason for this is that the brown-eyed gene is dominant, or stronger than the blue-eyed gene. The blue-eyed gene is recessive, or weaker than the brown-eyed one. Complex traits such as intelligence are governed by dozens of genes working in pairs.

A special pair of chromosomes decide whether the child will be female (a girl) or male (a boy). These special chromosomes are called sex chromosomes.

MULTIPLE BIRTHS

Sometimes a mother gives birth to two children at the same time. Such children are called twins. If the twins developed from two eggs that were fertilized at the same time, they are called fraternal twins. Fraternal twins do not have the exact same heredity. Their looks differ. And one can be a girl and the other a boy.

Some twins are identical. Others, such as the two boys at right, are fraternal.

In some cases the one fertilized egg splits into two parts, each of which becomes a baby. When this happens the babies share the same heredity and are called identical twins. These twins have the exact same heredity. Identical twins look the same. They are also of the same sex.

In rare cases a woman gives birth to more than two babies at a time. Three babies at once are

Four babies at a time are called quadruplets.

Baby pigs (left) and baby ducks (above) stay close to their mothers.

called triplets. Four at a time are quadruplets, and five are quintuplets. Many animals routinely give birth to more offspring at a time than that.

GENETIC DISEASES

Faulty genes can cause health problems. Several thousand diseases are caused at least partly by faulty genes. These are called genetic diseases, or hereditary diseases. Recently, scientists have found a new way to make drugs that combat several genetic diseases. They get bacteria to do it!

Using a method called *recombinant DNA*

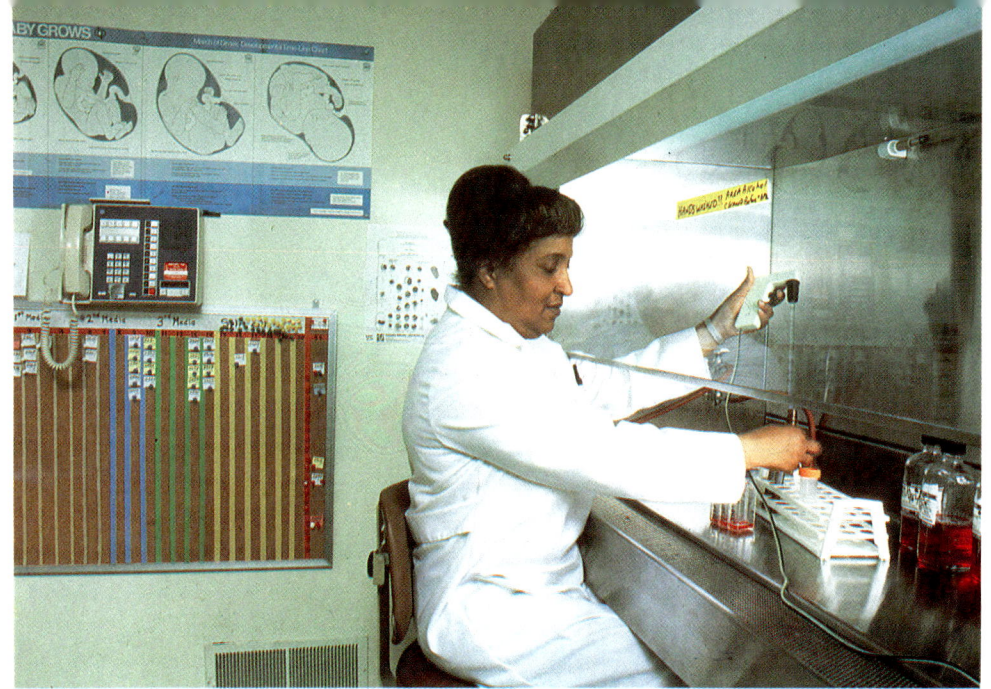

Scientists are making special drugs in laboratories that can be used to fight some genetic diseases.

technology, human genes have been placed in bacteria. The genes tell the bacteria to make certain substances lacked by sick people's bodies. A drug was first made in this way in 1982, when scientists used bacteria to make insulin, a substance lacked by many diabetic people. Since then, bacteria have been programmed to make several other drugs.

Doing things to genes to combat genetic and other problems is often called genetic engineering. Making drugs with bacteria and genes is the main type of genetic engineering today. But one day scientists may

A technician counts chromosomes using a microscope and a video display screen.

learn to operate on genes in people's bodies. They may be able to take out faulty genes, and replace them with good ones. Scientists have already done some gene transplants in animals.

Genes make people what they are. In the future genetic research may extend and improve the quality of life for all humans.

Wouldn't it be wonderful if doctors could replace genes that help cause cancer and heart disease with healthy genes? Doctors may even learn to remove genes that cause aging, so that people could live much longer. Much excitement lies ahead as we learn how to use the power of genetics to help humanity.

WORDS YOU SHOULD KNOW

bacterium (plural bacteria) (bak • TEER • ee • yum) — a one-celled organism

cells (SELLZ) — the smallest units of living matter; cells are units of which animals and plants are made

chromosomes (KROH • mo • sohmes) — thread-shaped structures containing large numbers of genes

DNA (deoxyribonucleic acid) (de • OX • ee • ry • bo • NOO • clee • ick) — the main genetic material

dominant gene (DOM • in • ent) — one that is stronger than a recessive gene

egg (EHG) — the female sex cell

environment (en • VY • ron • ment) — the surroundings of a plant or animal

females (FEE • mailz) — girls and women

fertilization (fer • til • ih • ZAY • shun) — the start of pregnancy

fraternal twins (fra • TER • nil TWINZ) — twins that developed from two eggs fertilized at the same time

genes (JEANS) — the units on chromosomes that determine heredity

genetic diseases (or hereditary diseases) (jen • ET • ik dih • ZEEZ • iz) — health problems caused at least partly by faulty genes

genetic engineering (jen • ET • ik en • jin • EER • ing) — the manipulation of genes to combat genetic problems

geneticists (jen • ET • ih • sists) — scientists who study heredity

heredity(hih•RED•ih•tee)—the passing of traits from parents to their young

identical twins(eye•DEN•tik•il TWINZ)—twins that developed from the same egg

instinct(IN•stinkt)—an inherited type of behavior

males(MAILZ)—boys and men

microscope(MIKE•roh•scope)—an instrument that makes small objects look bigger

nucleus(NOO•klee•uss)—the control center, near the middle of a cell, that contains the chromosomes with their genes

proteins(PRO•teenz)—substances, needed by all living things, that are made in cells

recessive gene(ree•SESS•ihv JEAN)—one that is weaker than a dominant gene

recombinant DNA technology(ree•KAHM•bin•int DNA tek•NAHL•ih•gee)—a method in which genes are cut and put together in new combinations; this has already been done to make several drugs

sex cells(SEX SELLZ)—female eggs and male sperm

sex chromosomes(SEX KROH•mo•sohmes)—a special pair of chromosomes that decide whether a child will be a girl or a boy

species(SPEE•ceez)—a type of plant or animal, such as human beings or dandelions

sperm(SPIRM)—the male sex cell

trait(TRAYT)—a characteristic (like blue eyes or a pointed nose)

INDEX

animals, 6, 8, 13, 15, 39
  cells of, 18
  gene transplants in, 43
bacteria, 6, 40-42
bacterium, 18
births, 7, 36
brains, 11, 22
brothers, 14
cats, 7, 13
cells, 15, 17-19
center of cell, 19
chemical differences, 24-25
chromosomes, 17, 20, 21-22, 32
"code of life, the," 24
deoxyribonucleic acid (DNA), 24
diabetes, 42
differences in DNA structure, 24
diseases, 40
dogs, 7, 11, 13
dominance of genes, 35
drugs, 41, 42
egg, fertilized, 32
environment, 14
experiments, pea plants, 16
eye color, 5, 25
father, cells from, 31-33
fraternal twins, 36
faulty genes, 40-45
genes, 17, 22-23, 40
  complexity of, 24-25
  dominance of, 35
  faulty, 40-45
  transplants, 43
genetic:
  diseases, 40-45
  engineering, 42
geneticists, 24
growth, human, 23, 32
hair, color of, 5
health problems, 40-45
height, 25
hereditary diseases, 40

heredity, 5, 6, 7, 22
humans, 8, 18-19, 21, 41
identical twins, 13, 37
insulin, 42
intelligence, 25, 35
laws, heredity, 6
living things, all, 6, 7, 9, 14, 18
looks, inherited, 5, 13, 36-37
Mendel, Gregor Johann, 15-16
mental ability, 11
microscopes, 16, 18
multiple births, 36
nucleus, 19
number, of chromosomes, 21, 32
  of genes, 25
parents, 5
pea plants, 16, 21
people, 8, 11, 12
personality, 13, 23
plants, 6, 8, 11, 13, 15, 18
proteins, 26
quadruplets, 39
qualities, special, 13
quintuplets, 39
recessive gene, 35
recombinant DNA, 40
reproduction, 6
resemblance, 6, 13
Schleider, Matthias, 15
Schwann, Theodor, 15
scientists, 15-17, 24, 40-43
sex cells, 31, 35
sisters, 14
size, inherited, 9
species, 9, 13, 20
sperm, 32
starfish, 9, 10
technology, recombinant DNA, 40-41
tomatoes, cells of, 21
traits, 5, 6, 13, 22-23, 33, 35
triplets, 38-39
twins, 13, 36, 37

About the author

Dennis Fradin attended Northwestern University on a partial creative scholarship and was graduated in 1967. His previous books include the Young People's Stories of Our States series for Childrens Press, and Bad Luck Tony for Prentice-Hall. In the True book series Dennis has written about astronomy, farming, comets, archaeology, movies, space colonies, the space lab, explorers, and pioneers. He is married and the father of three children.